For Margaret on the
Occassion of her
Graduation from LRNS.
love
Mum.

SCREAMING LIFE

A CHRONICLE OF THE SEATTLE MUSIC SCENE • PHOTOGRAPHS BY CHARLES PETERSON
INTRODUCTION BY MICHAEL AZERRAD • FOREWORD BY BRUCE PAVITT

HarperCollins*West*
An Imprint of HarperCollinsPublishers

pp. 1, 128 **Kurt Cobain.** *Seattle Center Coliseum, September 1992.*
p. 3 **Matt Lukin of Mudhoney.** *Hibernia, London. June 1990.*
pp. 4–5 **Stage diver at a Nirvana show.** *University of Washington, HUB Ballroom, January 1990.*

A TREE CLAUSE BOOK

HarperCollinsWest and the authors, in association with The Basic Foundation, a not-for-profit organization whose primary mission is reforestation, will facilitate the planting of two trees for every one tree used in the manufacture of this book.

SCREAMING LIFE: *A Chronicle of the Seattle Music Scene.* Copyright © 1995 by Charles Peterson and Michael Azerrad. All rights reserved. Printed in the United States of America. No part of this book may be used or reproduced in any manner whatsoever without written permission except in the case of brief quotations embodied in critical articles and reviews. For information address HarperCollins Publishers, 10 East 53rd Street, New York, NY 10022.

HarperCollins®, ®, and HarperSanFrancisco™ are trademarks of HarperCollins Publishers Inc.

Book design by Hank Trotter, Art Chantry, and Charles Peterson.

FIRST EDITION

Library of Congress Cataloging-in-Publication Data

Peterson, Charles
 Screaming Life : a chronicle of the Seattle music scene / Charles Peterson and Michael Azerrad—1st ed.
 ISBN 0-06-258640-8 (pbk.)
 1. Rock groups—Washington (State)—Seattle—Pictorial works.
 2. Grunge music—History and criticism. I. Azerrad, Michael. II. Title.
ML3534.P48   1995
781.66'09797'772—dc20   95-21041
                                                                                                                                      MN

95 96 97 98 99 ❖ RRD(W) 10 9 8 7 6 5 4 3 2 1

Dedicated to Kurt

Foreword *by Bruce Pavitt*

Charles Peterson is a cantankerous, opinionated, belligerent, cranky young man. He also shoots photos.

I've had the pleasure of knowing Charles since the mid-eighties, when we both kept winding up at the edge of the stage. I always wondered how anyone could hold a beer in one hand, take pictures with the other, and still manage to get kicked in the face. Night after night, if there was a show, Charles was there. Some photographers do it for the money. Somehow Charles ignored all of that and became successful anyway, spending his time doing something he believed in.

Musicians have always trusted Charles. His bluntness and candor are legendary; his blaring honesty has cost him some jobs and even lost him some "friends." But an artist knows that if Mr. Peterson is at a show it's because the band is good. Otherwise, he wouldn't waste his time. Musicians trust Charles, and they respect his integrity.

In a way, this brilliant, elephantine documentation of the developing Seattle music scene is nothing more than a family photo album. All of the characters on these pages have somehow influenced one another. They're all from a very particular time and place, and they reflect an organically developing community of artists and fans. There's a startling sense of connectedness to the images here. This is not a portfolio of random promotional assignments, as you would find with almost any other photographer in the entertainment business. Instead, this is something much more personal, much more intense, much more real. These images mean something.

Charles Peterson is more than a music fan, he's a fanatic. That's why no matter how popular the bands become or how large the venues get, Charles and his camera will always be found in the same place: at the edge of the stage.

Preface *by Charles Peterson*

A photography teacher once told me she couldn't regard my work as serious because the subject was rock and roll. I told her she was terribly mistaken and that I would prove her wrong, wrong, wrong. Well, here are 128 pages of proof.

I grew up in Bothell, Washington, a little place connected to a lot of other little places that make up the suburbs of Seattle. In 1980, at the age of sixteen, I discovered the first Clash album, and from that point on I was hooked on punk rock. At the time, I was a photographer for the high school newspaper and the yearbook and I was the school's one and only "punk rocker"; my shaved head and combat boots set me apart from everyone else. Imagine being harassed by the entire football team (egged on by the coaches) while trying to take their group photo—"Punk rock faggot! We're gonna kill you!"

Fortunately, Seattle was only half an hour away, an oasis where one could see a multitude of bands in a multitude of styles. To a sixteen year old, it seemed like a world revolution was under way. But all of my favorite bands were from elsewhere: England, New York, L.A., S.F., Cleveland, etc. Locally, nothing was truly unique or truly *ours*. There were some good bands, but they just seemed to be mimicking others. Granted, there was controversy to be had, this still being the early days of American punk (dyed-red hair was the exception, not the norm). Even I created a small stir by writing a review of the Fags, a local art punk outfit, for my school newspaper.

In my first month at the University of Washington, during the fall of 1982, I spotted this guy with a buzz cut, a big nose, Converse high-tops, and a Crass T-shirt in the dormitory lunchroom. Being desperate for friends, I stopped him and introduced myself. He turned out to be Mark Arm, guitar player in Mr. Epp and the Calculations, a truly indescribable band from the Eastside. We became great friends and, a year later, roommates.

Mark introduced me to Bruce Pavitt. Then Bruce introduced me to Kim Thayil, and so it went. Soon we had built up a circle of friends who were interested in playing, producing, promoting, and photographing this new brand of heavy guitar rock that would later be promoted as "grunge." The music's roots were deeply entwined in the shared experience of being the negative creep of the high school, and in the punk rock that got us through that. Before we knew it, we had a unified, albeit small, music scene that we could call our own.

Screaming Life is a collaboration among the musicians, the fans, and myself. It is a visual *impression* of a movement that is unique in the history of rock and roll. I am deeply indebted to fate for giving me such an outstanding group of bona fide characters to work with. Each one deserves to be famous in his or her own right. The fact that they *all* became famous is no real surprise. But the fact that they all came from the same place is. As the subtitle promises, *Screaming Life* is a chronicle of the Seattle music scene—but foremost it is simply a collection of my greatest hits, the very best of my work as a photographer. There is no way of escaping one's own history—my history, of both my life and my art, is inextricably linked to that of the Seattle music scene. Nirvana, Mudhoney, Soundgarden, Sub Pop, et al., changed my life; I hope in some small way I changed theirs.

I've tried to give an honest portrayal of honest music and its honest performance. There are no tricks here. Nothing is staged, no "four songs in I'm going to dive into the audience—here's the signal . . ." sort of thing. Everyone in this book is either a good friend or an acquaintance of mine (and of one another). We are all on the same wavelength. Unlike most of the countless thousands of other photos of these bands, these were taken here in their hometown, by a native, by someone who was there from the beginning.

These photos are not about the musicians' private lives (I don't want my private life exposed in a book, so why should they?). Instead, I've attempted to capture the private lives they brought *on stage*, as they bared their souls for us through rock and roll. With their furious, emotionally intense performances, they revealed to us much about themselves (and ourselves). Sometimes that turned out to be more than anyone expected. I wanted to reflect that catharsism in my photographs. I have, I hope, succeeded.

In assembling these photographs I chose from nearly 25,000 frames of film, not a simple task. In the process I had to divorce myself from many, many pictures. I apologize to the bands that didn't make the cut (there are many of you). Those musicians are just as integral to the story, and to my life, as the ones shown here.

My deepest regret is that Kurt isn't around to see the book. And Andy. And Jesse. And Mia. And Stephanie. Two weeks before Kurt's suicide, I bumped into him on Seattle's Capitol Hill. I mentioned that I was looking for a book deal. His face lit up, and his jaw set in that Popeye-with-a-smile way he had. "Allright! It's about time we get the real thing." He offered his help, gave me his new phone number, and then went on his way.

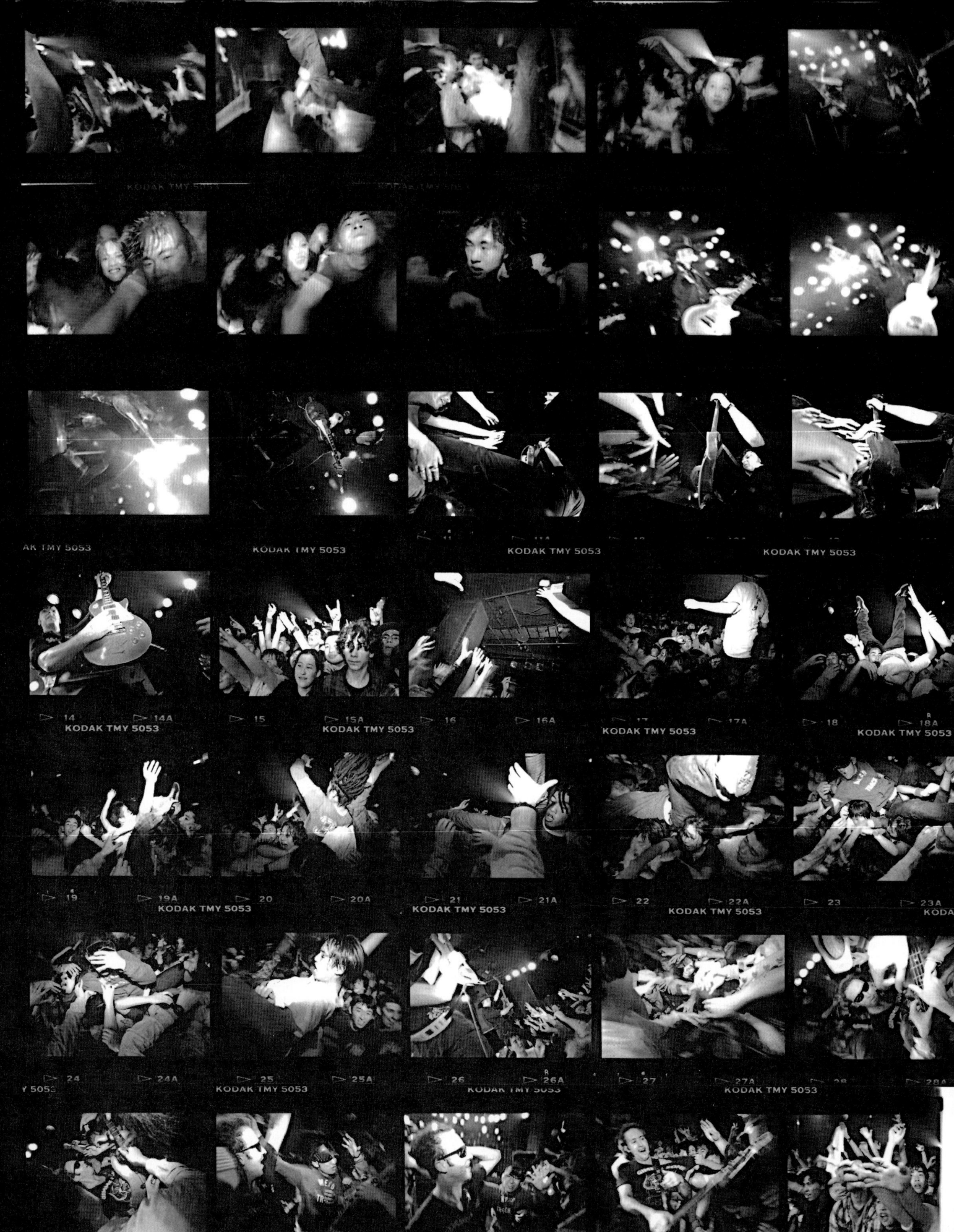

Introduction *by Michael Azerrad*

People often wonder why "Seattle" happened in Seattle. Of course, the phenomenon was founded on a miraculous concentration of truly amazing bands—Green River, Soundgarden, the Melvins, Nirvana, TAD, Mudhoney, and Pearl Jam, among many others—that made music that resonated profoundly with the youth of America and eventually the world.

But Seattle wouldn't have happened without the help of four very crucial individuals: Sub Pop chiefs Bruce Pavitt and Jonathan Poneman, producer Jack Endino, and photographer Charles Peterson. If Pavitt and Poneman were, respectively, the scene's right and left brains, then Endino was the ears and Peterson was the eyes. Pavitt's and Poneman's contributions are well known, but without Endino there would not have been a consistent sound for consumers to latch onto. And without Peterson there would be no consistent image.

"There was a group of people who really ended up being the unwitting parents, the people who birthed the scene," says Poneman. "And Charles is one of those people." Peterson belonged to the same social circle as the bands he photographed, but instead of a guitar, he had picked up a camera. Like playing rock music, photography is easy to learn but hard to master.

Just as none of the musicians were in it to get rich (well, maybe one or two were), Peterson didn't shoot bands because he thought the photos might be valuable some day—he shot them because photography was his artistic contribution to the musical community. "Charles represents the scene," says Pavitt. "Those photos defined what was going on every bit as much as the sound of the music." The fact that Peterson was even at those obscure early shows proved he was on the same wavelength as the musicians.

It's difficult to overestimate the vital role excellent photographs played in Sub Pop's wildly successful image-powered hype campaign. Besides being the perfect visual analogue to the music it documented, the sheer quality of Peterson's work made Seattle's underground rock that much more attractive to the people who bought the records.

Slam dancing to the Replacements at the Metropolis, 1983. *Left to right: Heather Lewis (Beat Happening): Slim Moon (Kill Rock Stars label); Mark Arm, Alex Shumway, and Steve Turner (Green River, Mudhoney); Ed Fotheringham (far right: the Thrown-ups).*

"Hearing the music on college radio was one thing," Pavitt acknowledges, "but those photos turned everybody into a star."

Screaming Life is ostensibly a historical account of the Seattle rock scene from its inception to the present. And yet many of the shots—the stage diver on the title page, for instance—could have been taken at almost any underground rock show in the late eighties or early nineties. These photos capture the spirit of the age even as they document a very specific place and time. They are proof positive that Seattle was the spiritual epicenter of the post-Reagan era zeitgeist, when the party was over and there was nothing left to do but revel drunkenly in the scraps that were left behind.

Legendary photographer Robert Frank once said, "There is one thing the photograph must contain, the humanity of the moment." Charles Peterson has made a career of capturing the humanity of the moment, plucking spontaneous beauty from the tumult of a rock show and revealing the honesty of its most unguarded instants. And as the photographs in this book demonstrate over and over again, rock's true glory lies in the fact that beauty and honesty are one and the same.

Of course, part of the allure of these photographs is that many of the people in them later became famous. But the shots of the less commercially successful bands, suffused with his distinctive artistic vision, are equally impressive.

A long time has elapsed since most of these photographs were taken, especially when viewed in rock terms. Now that the dust has settled a bit, they can be appreciated not only as reportage and effective marketing tools, but simply as wonderful works of art. So although most of the pictures were originally intended for use as photojournalism, they're well worth a second look, both to gauge Peterson's pivotal role in the Seattle phenomenon and to assess what shapes up as a formidable artistic achievement.

Freezing and framing moments that no one else noticed, Peterson found the remarkable in something as mundane as a bunch of relatively unknown bands playing in sweaty little clubs—and in the process, forged an entire aesthetic. Like Sub Pop, he seized on a small but meaningful set of attributes and amplified and repeated them, playing to the strength of the photographic medium and producing images that were easy to grasp yet were loaded with associations and portent.

*Seattle is widely regarded in rock and roll cir*cles as "Grungetown," but in reality, nothing could be further from the truth. Seattle is a gleaming, modern city largely populated by well-to-do young professionals who stride about town in spiffy business clothes during the workweek, then don teal blue Eddie Bauer jackets, jump in the Volvo, and drive off to the mountains to ski or hike. It was almost inevitable that a small rebel contingent would rise up against this starched white ocean of yuppiedom, the oppressive politeness of Seattle.

Bruce Pavitt in the Sub Pop office, circa 1988. *At the time, Sub Pop was a one-room operation; the door in the rear led to the bathroom, which doubled as storage for records. Sub Pop now has offices on three floors in the same building—that bathroom is now a hallway.*

Jonathan Poneman, left, coconspirator of Sub Pop, *with Everett True, the* Melody Maker *journalist who broke Sub Pop to England and, essentially, to the world. Seattle, 1992.*

There is at least one unstated rule of urban cool: never look like a hick. But the denizens of Seattle's underground directly appropriated the torn jeans, clunky shoes, and flannel shirts of Washington State's lumber country. That's because back in the eighties, provincial types were trying so hard to look sophisticated that the only way to distinguish (or was it alienate) yourself from them was, ironically, to look provincial. The scenesters grew their hair long as a reaction to the buzz-cut hardcore scene, as well as to the clean-cut yuppies who had overrun Seattle in the Reagan years.

This style—although nobody ever really considered it a style—was simply the way underground Seattle lived, and it's one of the aspects of the scene that Peterson so definitively captures in this series of photographs. But somewhere along the way, this antistyle—or rather, nonstyle—became product. Then media hype defined the style, prompted by the way the bands had already been defined by the Sub Pop propaganda machine, which was basically Pavitt and Poneman. And Charles Peterson.

Photograph a band with a strong, discernible, and consistent style and you help define the band. Peterson's work defined the look of the Seattle scene. But more importantly, it determined it; most people's mental image of the scene probably looks like a Charles Peterson photograph. He established a visual vocabulary that even other photographers rarely strayed from. There were a lot of imitators, but none could duplicate Peterson's vision.

So there was a snowball effect to what Peterson did. Sub Pop propaganda was a crucial cultural transmission line, and Peterson was not only documenting events but reinforcing and propagating an image. Other bands and fans emulated what they saw in these pictures. And then Peterson documented *them*. And so on and so on. Very quickly, chain wallets, ripped cardigans, baseball hats (preferably worn backward), and Doc Martens were all the rage.

Seattle rock dates back to at least the early sixties, but the phenomenon we know today had its beginnings in the late seventies and early eighties, when a handful of workmanlike hard-core bands and Anglophile new-wave and goth groups sustained what little scene there was in town. But new wave soon went the way of the skinny tie, hard-core became played out, and everyone realized goth sucked. Thanks to the cover band fad, local music began to wane badly. SEATTLE SCENE FOUND DEAD, an anonymous poster blared in 1984. By June of that year, the respected Seattle free monthly the *Rocket* ran a piece entitled "Who's Killing Seattle Rock and Roll?" "What this town needs is one band to blow us all away," wrote the *Rocket's* John Keister. "Just one band who can play some music that captures the imagination of the town, that would turn everything around."

Jack Endino outside Reciprocal Recording Studio in Fremont. *Jack recorded many of the early Sub Pop records here, including Nirvana's, Mudhoney's, and Soundgarden's debuts. 1989.*

Everybody fell back on the classics: cartoonish seventies hard rock like Alice Cooper, Kiss, and Black Sabbath, as well as hipper bands like the MC5 and Iggy and the Stooges. Meanwhile, literally adventurous touring bands like Big Black, Black Flag, the Replacements, the Butthole Surfers, Scratch Acid, Sonic Youth, and the Meat Puppets—all galvanic live acts—had started making the long trip up the coast to Seattle, where they were greeted by wildly appreciative audiences. The Seattle crowds were delighted that just about *any* band would show up in their long overlooked town. No one stood around with their arms crossed in a show-me gesture and, even better, lots of people were ripped on beer or the drug du jour, Ecstasy. In other words, they were an ideal audience.

But because of Seattle's repressive liquor laws, rock shows have traditionally been hassled by the police and fire departments, as they are to this day. The more bohemian types, who either lived or hung out in downtown Seattle, went underground and formed a tight network. A thriving basement/impromptu venue scene sprang up, promoted mostly by word of mouth. Like the region itself, the scene was isolated and developed its own quirky, inbred style: big, blunt, and nihilistic.

Most of the bands that helped ignite the scene were on the influential SST and Twin/Tone indie labels, whose bands typically wallowed in distortion, but the sound of Seattle underground music was also very much tied in with the place it came from. There's something about the Northwestern mentality that is very passive-aggressive. People don't like to talk directly to one another. You hear about stuff from friends of friends, or you're expected to pluck it out of thin air. So people vent through their music. Then there's the beverage syndrome. Seattle is renowned for two drinks: coffee and beer. When you guzzle java all day and then quaff glorious microbrewed suds all night, you're going to wind up playing music that's aggressive but sludgy, aka "grunge." And the city is surrounded by rugged mountains—the Cascades, the Olympics, and mighty Mount Rainier—all of which you can see from downtown (on the odd clear day). They make one feel distinctly primitive; Sub Pop's Jonathan Poneman once described grunge as "a backwoods yeti stomp."

Note also that the recording studios in town were not very sophisticated, so recorded music was bound to sound crude. And finally, there's the regional pride (not to mention sheer good taste) that has kept alive the memories of fiercely fuzzy early-sixties Northwest rockers such as the Wailers, the Kingsmen, and the Sonics.

Around late 1984, a tiny scene began to develop, populated mostly by University of Washington students. "It wasn't a confederacy of individuals whose sworn mission was to reinvent rock and roll," recalls Poneman. "It was just a bunch of people having a good time." Since they were of drinking age, they could hang out in—and play at—a small circuit of Seattle taverns. "There were two or three clubs and that was usually just one night a week," recalls Bruce Pavitt. "The Central Tavern on Saturday, the Vogue on Tuesday. Maybe the Rainbow Tavern. You'd tend to see the same people over and over again. And that's how the nucleus was really formed, the whole feeling of extended family."

A key part of that nucleus lived in a legendary abode known as the Room Nine House, so called because Ron Rudzitis of the psychedelic band Room Nine lived there, as did Danny Peters, drummer for Feast, a glam-goth band that was at one time the great white hope of the Seattle scene, and a photographer named Charles Peterson. Just down the block from the Rainbow, the Room Nine House became a regular after-show hangout. It was there that Bruce Pavitt, recently relocated from Olympia, noticed some live photographs Peterson had taken of his friends' bands and decided that yes, there could definitely be a big scene in Seattle.

It is here that Peterson's running visual narrative of the Seattle scene begins. At first, there seems to be about twenty people in the audience in those taverns, most of whom went on to become key players in the area music scene. Close inspection of some of the shots taken during this period reveals audience members such as Pearl Jam's Jeff Ament, Kill Rock Stars label cofounder Slim Moon, Mudhoney manager Bob Whittaker, even Mr. Lifto from the Jim Rose Circus Side Show.

A tremendous amount of mutual support was the key factor in getting the scene off the ground. "When I was photographing Green River, the members of Soundgarden were all around me," Peterson recalls. "When I was photographing Soundgarden, the members of Green River were slamming all around me. We all went and saw one another's bands."

Dan Peters drumming with Mudhoney. *Part of the backbone of the Seattle scene, Dan has played with Feast, Bundle of Hiss, Mudhoney, Screaming Trees, the Fastbacks, and Nirvana. The Vogue, 1988.*

Things went nationwide when Homestead, then one of the coolest indie labels in the country, released an EP by the coolest band in Seattle, the U-Men. "[U-Men lead singer] John Bigley taught everyone how to throw themselves around and go nuts," says Peterson. "The U-Men really were the first true grunge band."

Green River, who released the *Come On Down* EP on Homestead shortly thereafter, consisted of drummer Alex Vincent, guitarists Stone Gossard and Bruce Fairweather, and bassist Jeff Ament, a former Montana all-state basketball player. Lead singer Mark Arm named the band after a chain of serial killings then terrorizing the Northwest. "Mark's dark side was always the predominant feature of the band," says Art Chantry, renowned Seattle underground designer and a keen observer of the scene. "That right there was the signature of Green River." Arm, a college buddy of Peterson's and the scene's unofficial arbiter of cool, got Peterson started formally photographing rock bands when he asked him to shoot the cover photo for the *Come On Down* EP.

In April of 1986 came the epochal *Deep Six* compilation. Featuring the U-Men, Malfunkshun, the Melvins, Skin Yard, Green River, and Soundgarden (as well as photographs by Peterson), it is the Holy Grail of what was soon to be dubbed "grunge," a distorted miasma of guitars, sweat, and benign belligerence that was part punk and part outré seventies hard rock and metal, spiced with vestigial dollops of new wave and goth. Malfunkshun's over-the-top Black Sabbath/Kiss arena-rock bashing was bracingly preposterous. Skin Yard emitted a ponderous noise that suggested a goth Led Zeppelin, but Soundgarden was *unabashedly* Zeppelinesque—although where the homage left off and the satire began was anybody's guess. But perhaps the most grungy of them all was the Melvins, a trio whose stylized bludgeoning laid the sludgy bedrock of the sound of Seattle.

Screaming Trees with Donna Dresch *in their hometown of Ellensburg (above), summer of 1988; and a road-weary Trees backstage at the Paramount Theatre in 1993.*

Steve Mack, a native Seattleite who had traveled to London to sing with That Petrol Emotion, wrote home to his shutterbug friend Charles Peterson that summer: "What in the world are you doing there when there's so much happening here? I know damn well what you're doing. Are you sure it's worth it?"

Bruce Pavitt had published a fanzine called Sub Pop *in the Washington State capital of Olympia, exclu*sively featuring regional American indie rock, then began releasing cassettes of the bands he was writing about. In 1986 he put his money where his regional mouth was and released *Sub Pop 100*, a vinyl compilation of underground bands from around the country, including Sonic Youth, Big Black, and the Wipers, a brilliant Portland, Oregon, band that deeply influenced the entire Northwest scene. KCMU DJ, musician, and club show promoter Jonathan Poneman came on board a few months later, and in July of 1987 they released Green River's *Dry as a Bone* EP and a single by Soundgarden. Then came the Soundgarden EP *Screaming Life*, followed by a string of singles and the all-Seattle *Sub Pop 200*, virtually all of which featured Peterson's work on the cover.

Most indie labels gave the artists complete creative control when it came to album artwork, but Sub Pop was more heavy-handed. They wanted a consistent look, so they consistently used Peterson.

Sub Pop wisely gave the photographer little direction. Knowing a major talent when they saw one, they simply let Peterson's sensibility—which was the same as the one that created the music in the first place—determine how their bands would look. "I remember Bruce would go through Charles's pictures, trying to decide which one to use," says Poneman. "He'd say, 'Brilliant . . . brilliant . . . more brilliant.' And that's the one he'd pick. It wasn't like we said, 'We want them to look loose and yet rocking'—it was something that was just effortless."

At the time, a typical rock photo featured the entire band standing in front of a wall, posing. But Sub Pop wanted to convey the unique energy of their bands, even if it meant that a couple of members might not be in the picture. "That was unheard of," says Pavitt. "You just did not do that. But I would always fight for that. 'Where's the drummer?' 'Fuck the drummer, here's Chris Cornell, this is what's happening.'"

Sub Pop preferred live shots for both album art and promos, photographs that would get reproduced in magazines that couldn't afford to use their own photographer. "With us," Pavitt says, "it was, 'Here's Mudhoney rolling around on the floor because they can barely stand up.' That was our promo photo. And that really distinguished what we were doing from a lot of other labels."

A case in point was Peterson's Green River promo shot, taken for the *Rehab Doll* album. There were five people in the band but only three in the photo, and they were little more than blurry blobs. "You looked at this thing and you thought you were tripping, it was so distorted," says Pavitt. "I thought it was a very artful presentation." The logic was sound: mainstream rock magazines would never touch these bands, so why make a mainstream photo? Sure enough, the shot was picked up by countless fanzines, including the influential *Forced Exposure*.

Peterson was a perfect match for Sub Pop because he also preferred photographs of live performances, where Seattle rock was at its best. "The kind of photography that makes a lasting impression is of people just being themselves," he says. "And that's part of the reason I enjoy photographing people live. They're in another state—they're not aware of the camera, they're in their own adrenalin-charged world."

Nothing demonstrates Peterson's point better than his live photographs of Kurt Cobain. Even when Cobain is trashing his equipment, there's an almost childlike expression on his face, similar to that of a child who is intently destroying a toy. He's not grimacing in anger; he's just lost in that adrenalin-charged world.

Marvels of controlled chaos, Peterson's compositions have the same quality that makes the best live rock music exciting—the riveting tension between its sturdy basic structure and the very plausible possibility that it may all fly apart at any moment. "Charles caught the real spazzes like Mark Arm and Jeff Ament and Chris Cornell," says Soundgarden's Kim Thayil. "Even people who didn't move a whole lot, Charles was there when they did and he made it seem a lot more exciting. It was all about motion and action."

Peterson shot almost exclusively in black and white for several reasons. "There's a certain depth and a step back from reality with monochrome that is really appealing," he says. "Negative space is stronger and you can manipulate more after the fact, too." And sure, Peterson's favorite photographers—Garry Winogrand, Henri Cartier-Bresson, and Diane Arbus—shot in black and white. Most punk rock photography was in black and white simply because the low-budget indie labels, magazines, and fanzines couldn't afford color. Like so many other aspects of punk, poverty begat an entire aesthetic, and Peterson plugged right into it. Even his equipment was relatively low-rent, while his decision to adopt a grainy, Blue Note Records–style look became a lot easier when he got a bunch of high-speed Kodak T-Max film for a cheap price.

Another of Peterson's trademarks was a blurring effect that made it appear as if the photographer were painting with light. "It's just something you do with the camera—you leave the shutter open and the flash goes off," he says. "People have been doing it for years. But with the blurs in my photos, there was always control. I controlled it. It's not accidental." The blurs also re-created the way a typical Seattle show was experienced. Just as the hallucinatory artwork from the late-sixties San Francisco scene simulated an LSD trip, Peterson's smeary photographic vision simulated the inebriated ambience of the Seattle scene or, as Peterson puts it, "the experience of falling down with a can of Schmidt in your hand."

"His photos made you feel like you were right there, inches away from these people," says Pavitt. "And you would see the fans reaching out to touch the stars, whereas at arena rock shows, you didn't see that." Peterson's photographs did give the viewer an almost palpable sensation of being in the pit, watching the show. "I wanted my photos to portray how it feels when you're standing there and a band is going off in your face," says Peterson. Part of the trick was using his mainstay lens, a 24 mm Nikkor, which gives a perspective similar to that of the human eye.

But the real secret was Peterson's approach. Peterson photographs like a great rock musician plays music—with physicality and passion. (This is a guy whose arms are tattooed with the logos for Leica and Hasselblad cameras.) It's impossible to convey precisely what it was like to be at

The "blurry" Green River photo *used as a publicity shot by Sub Pop. The Town Pump, Vancouver, B.C., 1986.*

those shows, but it was exciting to watch Peterson try, and the way he tried communicates almost as much as the pictures he took.

While other photographers would camp out at a safe distance from the stage and use a telephoto lens, Peterson would wade right into the middle of the mosh pit and dance, stopping occasionally to snap a picture. "I always had to be up front," he says. "That was the best perspective. I had to be where the action was happening—I was never satisfied with standing in the wings. The neck of their guitar was usually inches away from my face, so there was a certain danger. And yeah, I got smacked by a guitar or a microphone a few times. It's just part of it."

"A lot of photographers shooting the same thing wouldn't risk getting a boot in the face," says Pavitt. "Charles was always there." Along with a lot of bruises and broken equipment, Peterson got something that was unique and true, what live rock music is all about: a commotion of hair, sweat, guitars, drums, and wires, which he juggled using classical compositional elements like torsion, symmetry, and texture, all rendered in glorious black and white.

Somehow he managed, in the midst of the chaos, to snap photographs that are works of art. And he did this by almost literally shooting from the hip, producing miracles of instantaneous composition. "It's like the difference between shooting a formal portrait and a land war," says Peterson. "The most important thing is the quickness of your reflex."

The proof sheet is literally that—proof of Peterson's gift. Any suspicion that his photographs are merely happy accidents is decisively erased by the uncanny consistency of the shots on the proof sheet. And in what amounts to photographic bravado, Peterson always printed his photos with the borders intact. His composition was so impeccable that the pictures didn't even need to be cropped.

"The bands just sort of fell into your camera," Peterson says a bit modestly. "You'd put it in front of your face and everything would fall into place." Of course, it wasn't quite that easy. Like all photographs, Peterson's involved a degree of luck, but with him it was skilled luck. As Brooklyn Dodgers manager Branch Rickey once said, "Luck is the residue of design." Peterson had a knack for putting himself in such a position that if chance did smile upon him, he'd be ready.

How did Peterson get himself in the right place at the right time? "Drinking a lot," he cracks. "That, my trusty 24 mm lens, and sharp elbows." Actually, Peterson had an advantage: he'd seen these performers many times before, and they were friends. He knew when they did certain moves just because he'd seen them so many times. And sometimes he just intuitively sensed when something great was about to happen—a smashed guitar, a swan dive into the crowd, or maybe even a guy playing while standing on his head.

That intuition stemmed from Peterson's shared sensibility with the bands he shot. His photographic style was the visual version of what was called "grunge." The photographs were lyrical and yet blurry, grainy, and bursting with brute force. It was like Peterson was shooting with a fuzzbox on his lens.

Later, as the moshing of ever-larger crowds got too intense even for him, he began shooting from the side of the stage, which often meant the audience was in the picture even more than before—another Peterson trademark. It's always been a premise of punk that the people on stage and the people in the audience are peers. And in that egalitarian spirit, Peterson's photographs invariably included the audience as much as the bands. "As far as the excitement went, it was half and half," he says. "The audience was just as exciting as the band on stage." And the two often intermingled, as the band waded into the audience or the audience used the stage as a diving board.

New York–based photographer Michael Lavine, a college friend of Pavitt's, took many of Sub Pop's cover shots. But Lavine's photos, although classic in their own way, were very "New York"; polished, posed, often using intentionally garish lighting, they are very exciting photographs of rock bands. In contrast, Peterson's shots conveyed a vivid, all-important sense of time and place.

And Peterson's work was on virtually every early Sub Pop release. Even when Lavine did the cover, there was always a photo by Peterson in the CD insert—no explanatory text, just the photo. So even if it was slick on the outside, it was definitely gritty on the inside.

Kurt Cobain conversing with Kim Gordon *when Sonic Youth, supporting Neil Young, played the Seattle Center Coliseum. 1991.*

Although they all got lumped together under the grunge tag, the Seattle bands didn't sound completely alike. TAD didn't rock in the same way Mudhoney did, and Nirvana didn't resemble Green River, but there was definitely a house sound to Sub Pop, largely due to producer Jack Endino. Working out of Chris Hanszek's Reciprocal Studios, located in a tiny building in the Seattle suburb of Ballard, Endino soon became known for his loud recordings with crunch and, almost as importantly, his reasonable rates. Among countless other recordings, Endino produced such seminal Seattle records as Mudhoney's *Superfuzz Bigmuff*, the Screaming Trees's *Buzz Factory*, Soundgarden's *Screaming Life*, TAD's *God's Balls*, Green River's *Dry as a Bone*, and Nirvana's debut album, *Bleach*.

As part of their master plan to make the Seattle scene seem more substantial than it was, Sub Pop consciously set out to make Peterson and Endino stars in their own right. Sub Pop singles rarely listed the musicians' names, but they always credited Peterson and Endino. The reasoning was that the endless thank-you lists on major-label records were a dead giveaway that the bands had to deal with reams of corporate bureaucracy in order to get their records made. So Sub Pop never credited more people than absolutely necessary. And through sheer repetition, they deified those who were.

Roughly speaking, Bruce Pavitt was the "Sub"—the underground hipster—and Jonathan Poneman was the "Pop"—the more melodic, populist side of the label. Pavitt was Mudhoney, Poneman was Nirvana, and both were equally crucial; while Pavitt focused on the label's image, Poneman concentrated on business. The Sub Pop boys had made a science of indie-rock promotion. Pavitt even had a college degree in it.

Their stated goal: "to decentralize pop culture."

Pavitt and Poneman loved the idea of regionality. People in England and, indeed, all over Europe, had an intense allegiance to their soccer teams; a similar demographic followed rock music. A regional allegiance, they astutely recognized, fulfilled some basic human need. And besides, regional labels from Motown (Detroit) to Factory (Manchester) had made the greatest music. So they played up the Seattle/Northwest angle.

The two men also had a heartfelt belief that New York and Los Angeles shouldn't have a monopoly on the production and dissemination of popular culture. Places like Memphis and New Orleans, for instance, were the cradles of rock and roll. More recently, Pavitt and Poneman had witnessed the explosion of the Minneapolis sound, spearheaded by the Twin/Tone label, and the market dominance of the southern California punk label SST. Both scenes contributed musically and visually (the flannel shirt, torn jeans, and long, unwashed hair) to the Seattle scene.

Sub Pop systematically set about fashioning an identity for the nascent Seattle scene by being consistent—signing similar but not quite identical-sounding bands, employing the same producer (Endino) at the same studio (Reciprocal), and using the same art direction (Pavitt, usually with designer Jane Higgins) and the same photographers (Peterson and Michael Lavine) to create a uniform look. "What Jonathan and I were trying to do," says Pavitt, "was take what was there and magnify it and turn it into mythology." Although not on the same commercial scale, it was as brilliantly calculated as anything accomplished by Brian Epstein, Berry Gordy, or Malcolm McLaren.

"We're using a precedent set by Tamla/Motown and Stax, where you have the scene that is being born in a particular region and then you just have a machine that you use to refine and perfect your product," Poneman told *Pulse* magazine in 1989. "All of a sudden there are all these bands coming out of this part of the world, there's good press, it's romantic. Everybody likes the idea that there is this burgeoning, happening scene somewhere in the world. If you're a teenage kid living in Dullsville, U.S.A., maybe someday you can go to Seattle and join a rock band and maybe play the Central."

Mark Arm and Matt Lukin of Mudhoney *avoiding the lines to the restrooms before taking the stage. Bristol University, U.K., October 1992.*

People bought the regional concept—literally. Sub Pop wanted to create the sense of an invasion, like the British Invasion, when people bought just about anything that came from England. The idea worked, and soon people were buying anything that came from Seattle. And lo and behold, most of it was quite staggeringly good.

It all started in August of 1988 with the Mudhoney single "Touch Me I'm Sick" (appropriately enough, the track begins with an authentic Seattle beer belch). With Mark Arm's Iggy-fied howl and the elegantly thuggish rhythm section buttressing a nasty broken-record fuzz guitar riff, the song became the opening war cry of the Seattle Invasion. Sonic Youth, indiedom's reigning royalty, sat up and took notice, talking up Mudhoney whenever they could and even taking them on tour, which intensified the New York band's already close connection with Sub Pop and the Seattle scene. There would be other honorary Seattleites: L.A.'s L7, Babes in Toyland, and Hole (Hole eventually relocated to Seattle); Cincinnati's Afghan Whigs; England's Billy Childish; Austin's Reverend Horton Heat; and Denver's Fluid. Most of them shared a stylistic affinity with the Sub Pop posse, and all recorded for Sub Pop.

Because Seattle is a magnet for artistic outcasts from the entire Northwest region, there were more members of the extended family nearby. Olympia's Beat Happening had a naive, childlike sound that inspired many Seattle bands; leader Calvin Johnson ran K Records, a visionary label whose D.I.Y. (Do-It-Yourself) approach was a key inspiration for Sub Pop. The mighty Screaming Trees, from Ellensburg, in the cultural no-man's-land of eastern Washington, had already made a couple of fine albums for SST before Sub Pop even existed. TAD, Seattle's early odds-on favorite to break into national prominence, came from Boise, Idaho. The Melvins and their musical progeny, Nirvana, were from the unlikely redneck bastion of Aberdeen, a dreary lumber and fishing town on the Washington coast.

As the scene began to reach critical mass, taverns like the Central, Rainbow, and Ditto were all thriving on local bands. With no major-label talent scouts (known in the industry as A&R people) poking around town, it was just friends playing for friends. Bands like Swallow, Blood Circus, H-Hour, and Bundle of Hiss came and went, and along with the household names of today, they participated in a perpetual game of musical chairs, mostly involving the same pool of about forty musicians. Although the Seattle family tree has surprisingly few members, it takes a computer database (which really exists) to sort it all out.

Nirvana's last photo shoot with drummer Chad Channing (right). *"I hate white paper backgrounds," Kurt informed me, so I offered him a can of spray paint and without hesitation he added the plus and minus signs. May 1990.*

Early on, there was an anything-goes attitude. "You can't really underestimate how loose things were," says Pavitt. "It's not like now, when everybody is very self-conscious because who knows, there might be an MTV camera there. Back then, people were constantly taking that risk, making fools of themselves and doing things that bordered on the irresponsible. Every time the Thrown-ups played, it was a twisted, amazing show."

Much has been made of the generational scream that emanated from Seattle, but looking through this book, one is struck by how funny the bands were. From sarcasm to sight gags, from the biting rants of underground Seattle's poet laureate Steven Jesse Bernstein to the propensity of Mudhoney's Matt Lukin for dropping his trousers on stage, humor was and still is part and parcel of the Seattle scene.

Ed Fotheringham, "singer" of the Thrown-ups, sometimes sported his Saran Wrap zit suit, which squirted pus-loads of shaving cream when poked with a broken drumstick. Malfunkshun's Andrew "Landrew the Love God" Wood would hit even the tiniest stage wearing stacked heels and whiteface and holler "Helloooo Seattle!" as if addressing a crowd at the Kingdome. Under the watchful gaze of Nirvana's legendary "Elvis Cooper" wall hanging, Kurt Cobain often ended a show by hurling his frail little body into the drum set.

The scene was full of inside jokes—visual, verbal, and musical—because this was supposed to be fun, not self-consciously arty and pretentious like the East Coast indie bands, not preachy and strict like hard-core. So it was all a big laugh. But when the bands took the stage, the fun became serious. The music fed off the humor. Peterson caught that.

Like most rock scenes (until recently), Seattle was a man's, man's, man's world. There were only a few major female-fronted bands, notably Seven Year Bitch, the Gits, Dickless, the Fastbacks, and L7. The first two were set back by the tragic, untimely deaths of Stephanie Sargent and Mia Zapata, respectively. But both groups forged bravely ahead, and Seven Year Bitch eventually landed a major-label deal, as did L7. The Fastbacks have made album after album of joyous pop-punk right up to the present; the visionary Dickless broke up before the rest of the world caught up to them. These bands clearly helped to inspire the vastly increased numbers of women playing rock music in the nineties.

Several women played pivotal roles in pioneering the Seattle scene, including KCMU music director Faith Henschel, who laid the groundwork for the major-label gold rush in 1987 by making a compilation tape of Seattle bands including Skin Yard, Soundgarden, Room Nine, Pure Joy, and Chemistry Set, and sent it off to key A&R people. The title of the tape: *These Bands Will Make Money*. Then there was Soundgarden manager Susan Silver, *Backlash* editor Dawn Anderson, and Feast bassist/Sub Pop designer Jane Higgins.

"Punk scenes are very female-influenced in the beginning—but as they become successful, when money enters the picture, women are forced out," observes designer Art Chantry. "It happened in this scene, too." As Peterson's photos attest, even the number of women in the audience dwindled as time went on and the mosh pit became a roiling vat of testosterone.

Still, plenty of women bought the records, and both genders seemed to be intrigued by what little sex appeal grunge had to offer. There was a latent homoeroticism to the Seattle scene; for one thing, shows basically became hordes of sweaty, bare-chested men banging into each other. Fluid lead singer John Robinson (who now works as a model) attracted his own sub-crowd of rapt young heterosexual men, while Soundgarden's Chris Cornell liked to show off his pecs and washboard stomach. On the cover of the *Screaming Life* EP, he's shirtless, wearing a ribbon in his hair. "I got a lot of shit for using a photo like that," says Pavitt. "I was basically saying, 'This is homoerotic and I'm going to push that a little bit.' And ooh boy, a lot of guys got really uncomfortable with that."

Green River broke up in 1987, and in retrospect it's easy to see why. The band was a microcosm of the two disparate visions within the scene. It was Hanoi Rocks vs. Iggy Pop, the difference between putting on makeup and playing tricky guitar licks or donning pegged jeans and high-tops and baring your soul, between major-label dreams and indie cred. Singer Mark Arm went on to co-found the brilliant garage punk band Mudhoney with early Green River guitarist Steve Turner, former Feast and Bundle of Hiss drummer Danny Peters, and ex-Melvin Matt Lukin. Jeff Ament and Stone Gossard formed a glammy new group with Andrew Wood, Greg Gilmore, and Bruce Fairweather, and called it Mother Love Bone, a reference to a particularly impressive erection.

Tragically, Wood died of a heroin overdose on March 19, 1990, just days before the band was to tour its much ballyhooed debut album on PolyGram. A devastated Seattle musical community held a wake at the Paramount Theatre. Gossard and Ament eventually formed a new band with drummer Dave Krusen, guitarist Mike McCready, and a San Diego surfer named Eddie Vedder on vocals, and called it Pearl Jam, a reference to semen.

My last photo shoot *with Nirvana. August 1993.*

After being pursued for two years by as many as a dozen labels, Soundgarden finally relented and signed with A&M in 1988. The major-label Pandora's box was now open, but Sub Pop still ran the show.

"Sub Pop believes there are brilliant artists in every community," read one early press release. "Linking these artists to the media is the trick." It was a trick they pulled off brilliantly. In 1989, the label took a big but calculated gamble and paid for writers from the various English music weeklies—*Melody Maker*, the *NME*, and *Sounds*—to fly to Seattle and check out the bands. The writers, jazzed as much by the oceans of local brew that were funneled down their desperately parched throats as they were by the music itself, raved.

The Brits loved this ultra-American music, although their condescension was all too apparent in their gleeful descriptions of the stereotypical Northwest lumberjack mentality. They were delighted that Tad Doyle was a 300-pound former butcher from Boise (conveniently overlooking the fact that Doyle also had a degree in music from the University of Idaho), beside themselves with ecstasy when informed that Nirvana's Kurt Cobain had grown up in a trailer park. Happy to play along with the joke, Doyle posed with a chain saw for photographers from weeklies. From then on, Sub Pop and the hype-fueled English weeklies fed off each other ravenously, as Peterson's Siamese twin–like photo of Poneman and English music journalist Everett True so slyly intimates.

Then again, there *was* a dumb side to Seattle rock that one *Sounds* article dubbed "transcendental mindlessness." Writer Jonathan Gold called it "art music for people who instinctively hate art." In the mid-eighties, the East Coast–centered push to mainstream the avant-garde was becoming incomprehensible to the masses. Poneman and Pavitt repeatedly expressed their disdain for the East Coast art school approach of performers like Talking Heads and Laurie Anderson, which they insisted was not rock and roll but "some weird arty shit that might be appreciated in the year 2000." But did Pavitt and Poneman succeed in making the artsy-elite indie rock scene more populist? Or did they help make populist music more arty?

Mia Zapata of the Gits. *RCKNDY, January 1993.*

As things progressed, the infrastructure of the Seattle scene became more and more hospitable to making and promoting music. New clubs were opening up all over town. The free weekly *Backlash* wrote exclusively about local bands, and KCMU played their music. The larger *Rocket* also strongly supported the local scene (as well as supplying a key musician's want ads section). It also supported Peterson, whose work constantly graced the paper's pages.

Sub Pop's Lamefest '89, a bill featuring TAD, Nirvana, and Mudhoney at Seattle's venerable old Moore Theatre, was a crucial turning point—local bands had never sold out the Moore before. Obviously, more people were into this music than just the original crowd of college students drinking their tuition money away in two or three small dives. A lot of kids were coming in now, mostly from the suburbs, but at least they were hip kids, as opposed to frat jocks who wanted to go out and kick ass. *They* moved in a little later.

But the fact was that outsiders were coming in and aping the rituals without really understanding what they meant. Ironically, while those outsiders provided the money that allowed the musicians to continue to do their work, they also diluted and homogenized the community. The original scenesters were simply getting older and were going out less often; instead of hanging around Seattle and playing for each other, trading records, and discussing them over a pint (or three) of Red Hook, the bands were now out on the road.

In this book, the double-page spreads of the audience mark the passage of time, acting practically as chapter headings. As Peterson's photographs so amply document, the crowds got bigger and bigger; the bands outgrew the tiny taverns they once played and graduated to larger venues where younger fans could attend. The gigs got more crowded, crazier. Little by little, the bands became more and more distanced from their audience.

By the end of 1990, no one, not even Pavitt and Poneman, could possibly imagine things going any further. A&R people from the major labels had been staking out Seattle for a couple of years now, but nobody was expecting anything particularly momentous from newly signed bands like the Posies, Alice in Chains, and Screaming Trees.

Then, on September 21, 1991, DGC released Nirvana's landmark album, *Nevermind*, and the whole thing got bigger than anyone could comprehend. Seattle became a frenzied feeding ground for the record labels, the media, even the fashion industry, and the attention showed no signs of letting up.

Pavitt and Poneman had made it all up—and the fantasy had become far too real. Suddenly, it wasn't so fun anymore. "That was a weird, sad period," Peterson recalls. "A lot of people felt left behind. Everyone wanted to be successful but in typical Seattle style, no one really wanted to be that big of a deal." A&R execs from every major label were flocking to Seattle and desperately scooping up whatever bands they could find. Bands even moved to Seattle from all over the country to try to make it. The media frenzy had ratcheted up several levels, making a quantum leap from the underground press to big features in mainstream national magazines like the *New Yorker* and *Rolling Stone*.

Film director Cameron Crowe (*Say Anything*) rolled into town and made *Singles*, a romantic comedy that used the Seattle grunge scene as a backdrop. Members of Pearl Jam appeared as costar Matt Dillon's band, Citizen Dick. Seattle scenesters roundly panned the film for being somewhat lacking in the authenticity department, and *Singles* did lackluster box office. But the soundtrack—featuring Pearl Jam, Alice in Chains, Mudhoney, and Screaming Trees, among others—went platinum.

Miraculously, Sub Pop had achieved its goal. The music industry had been decentralized. As the crowning achievement of rock's grassroots revolution, the Seattle phenomenon had at least hobbled the prevailing industry hegemony. Now the major labels had to pay attention to what kids really thought was cool, rather than force-feeding contrived music to the masses. Of course, force-feeding is still the predominant method of promotion, but things had changed at least slightly. Here was good music that spoke to a new consumer demographic; now that the baby boomers were spending their money on minivans, white wine, and exercise machines, the music industry finally realized that attention must be paid to the twentysomethings.

Just as grunge tore down the pancaked facade of "hair farmer" rock, Peterson's photographs demystified the look of rock music. With few barely notable exceptions, the Seattle scene boasted little in the way of pretty faces. These were not

An early show by Alice in Chains (top). *The Central Tavern, 1990.* **Ed Fotheringham (bottom),** *the Thrown-ups, modeling the famous zit suit. The Off Ramp, 1991.*

glamour shots by any stretch of the imagination. By concentrating on live shows and very casual group portraits, Peterson shot bands the way they were experienced, not the way they were marketed (of course, that very approach eventually became the way they were marketed). That honesty coincided with the music and the times. Pretty faces signaled artifice. People wanted authenticity.

And in a larger sense, Peterson's black-and-white shots of regular people rocking out in small clubs perfectly symbolized a downscaling that was a nineties touchstone, a make-do ethos that's manifested itself in everything from the lo-fi trend in indie rock to recycling—and has become more and more prevalent as the decade wears on.

After Nevermind, Peterson was basically documenting the aftermath of a nuclear explosion. But the aftermath was merely the beginning. Along with Nirvana, Soundgarden, Alice in Chains, and Pearl Jam became some of the biggest bands on the planet. Millions of people around the world suddenly became aware of what had been happening in Seattle for at least five years.

Although Peterson, like all great photographers, had physically been getting closer and closer to his portrait subjects, his stage shots remained as revealing as any intimate close-up. From the time of the 1992 Reading Festival and beyond, there is a tremendous amount of physical space around the bands, whether it's vast stretches of stage or huge patches of clear sky.

In the old days, shows at places like the Rainbow or the Central blurred the line between audience and performer; these new shows, however, were definitely a matter of Us and Them. Kurt Cobain looks virtually alone on the Reading stage. He had long since abandoned his traditional swims into the audience because people had started going through his pockets.

Before 75,000 people at a free show in Seattle's Magnusson Park in September of 1992, Pearl Jam performed on what looked more like a gigantic pedestal than a stage.

Some made the leap to international stardom more easily than others. They could adjust to the simple fact that the rock world is divided into two types of people: those who think of their heroes as peers, and those who want their heroes to be unapproachable. The former tend to go in for underground rock; the latter largely comprise the mainstream. As many Seattle bands went from obscurity to worldwide fame, some could endure and even enjoy the adulation and some couldn't. And it's apparent in Peterson's photographs. Chris Cornell's pectoral muscles seemed to swell with every unit sold; in Peterson's remarkable series of photographs of a pajama-clad Kurt Cobain, he looks like he has a bad case of the flu.

There was a benign little aftershock during a December 1993 Sub Pop package tour of Japan, which featured beloved Seattle pop-rockers the Fastbacks, a brilliant band that predated the Seattle explosion and will probably outlive it. Also along for the ride were Japanese punkers Supersnazz and two members of Sub Pop's young new breed: the Supersuckers and Seaweed.

Belatedly, Sub Pop had become a massive hit in the Land of the Rising Sun. There were packed, screaming autograph sessions after shows, crowds of young girls swooning over Eddie Supersucker. But this time, Pavitt and Poneman could take it in stride. There were more important things now, like baby daughters. The bands, most of whom had either been unjustly denied massive fame or seemed poised to receive it, lapped it up.

It was one last bit of joy before disaster struck. In early April of 1994, Kurt Cobain took his own life. Once again, the city became an instant media encampment, but this time there was nothing to cover but stunned grief. The hype machine had run amok, and it had proven fatal. Seattle was never the same after that.

Still, the town's days as a breeding ground for excellent rock bands are far from over. Perhaps the most dramatic and inspiring example is the Foo Fighters, a band led by former Nirvana drummer Dave Grohl and featuring guitarist Pat Smear, who had joined Nirvana just before Cobain died. Months before their debut album came out, the astounding band was the talk of the music industry; a couple of Northwest surprise shows had people lined up around the block. And latter-day Seattle has spawned other fantastic new bands such as Sunny Day Real Estate, Violent Green, and Silkworm. Meanwhile, the old guard has been making even deeper and deeper inroads into the belly of the music industry beast—Pearl Jam's *Vitalogy* sold nearly a million copies in its first week of release in 1995, the same year that Soundgarden won a Grammy for Best Heavy Metal Band.

Frances Bean Cobain with her mother, *Courtney Love, next to the collage Kurt made in their living room for the back cover of In Utero. April 1993.*

What had begun as an unspoiled little musical community, just a small circle of peers having fun, ended up being a ubiquitous and pervasive arm of the international culture industry. It's tempting to mourn that process, that loss of innocence, but that's a little like mourning the very process of growing up and getting older. Documenting life as it passes by, and the humanity of its moments, is one of the great strengths of photography. And that's all that Charles Peterson is really doing in these pages—capturing his own screaming life.

SCREAMING LIFE

John Bigley of the U-Men (far left), *who were the punk godfathers to the Seattle "grunge" scene. Their intense live shows influenced a generation of Seattle musicians still finding their feet. Tom Price (right) would later play in Gas Huffer. Oddfellows Hall, 1985.*

Green River's first photo session—*also the first time I photographed a posed band. Left to right: Jeff Ament, Mark Arm, Stone Gossard, Steve Turner, and Alex Shumway. 1985.*

Tom Mick of Feast (left) and Bruce Pavitt of Sub Pop (right). *A typical scene from the early days—watching their/your friends go insane on the stage of some local club. Feast, now long disappeared into obscurity, opened this particular show for Soundgarden at the Central Tavern some Saturday night in 1987.*

Mark Arm (far left) *leans into a young Soundgarden at the Ditto Tavern, an incredibly tiny Seattle venue that was one of the earliest outlets for the new crop of bands. Note Kim Thayil without a beard (left). 1985.*

The flamboyant Landrew the Love God, *aka Andrew Wood, in the legendary Malfunkshun; his brother, Kevin, is at left. Malfunkshun were a unique blend of glam, space, metal, and punk rock. Landrew would later front Mother Love Bone. The Central Tavern, 1986.*

Green River shakes the Ditto Tavern, *where they were practically the house band in late 1985 and early 1986.*

Green River at the Town Pump in Vancouver, B.C. *At this particular show, the style of my live photographs began to take on a life of its own; the blur suddenly became an integral element of expressing the action. Mark Arm (center) was the dark side of Green River. 1986.*

Soundgarden (right) at the Central Tavern in 1987. *A classic example of how the gap between audience and band was being constantly broken down at these explosive early shows.*

Sub Pop Sunday at the Vogue with Soundgarden sometime in 1987. The cover of their debut EP Screaming Life.

Mudhoney: *Matt Lukin (below) wielding his bass at the University of Washington HUB Ballroom in early 1989. It was used in the inner gatefold of only the first thousand copies of their single "You Got It (Keep It out of My Face)"—an instant collector's item for my photography alone. Mark Arm and Steve Turner (right) pile into each other on the stage of the Central Tavern in the summer of 1988. This photo was used for the cover of their debut EP Superfuzz Bigmuff. Mudhoney at the Central (overleaf), only several frames of film on from the Superfuzz Bigmuff cover.*

Gary Lee Conner and Mark Lanegan of the Screaming Trees. *Mark Lanegan told me this was his favorite photo of the Trees. It summed up everything he felt about the band. I felt incredibly honored by his compliment. The Moore Theatre, 1989.*

Mudhoney (above) at the infamous Boxing Club. *1988.*

Andrew Wood (overleaf) and Mother Love Bone *in the Pioneer Square loft I shared with Bruce Fairweather (bottom left). It was a very casual shoot, like most of my photo shoots in those days, with the band coming over for a few (or many) beers before we would (possibly) get around to taking some pictures. Andrew was a supremely kind person; I think that is reflected here. 1988.*

The first time I met Nirvana, *we rode around one sunny day in their trashed van listening to the Shocking Blue (whose "Love Buzz" Nirvana covered on their first single) looking for locations in the countryside—this was the last of the day. After meeting them, I was a diehard Nirvana fanatic. Left to right: Chad Channing, Krist Novoselic, Kurt Cobain. Bainbridge Island, Washington, 1988.*

TAD *during the video shoot for "Woodgoblins." Tad belied his backwoods image by confessing he had never used a chain saw before; he quickly became a natural with it. Left to right: Kurt Danielson, Gary Thorstensen, Tad Doyle, and Steve Weid. Hood Canal, Washington, 1989.*

TAD. *University of Washington HUB Ballroom, 1988.* **Krist Novoselic and Kurt Cobain** *(overleaf) from a show in the same place, same year.*

L7's music and attitude *were more kindred to what was happening in the Pacific Northwest than in their hometown of Los Angeles. Bassist Jennifer Finch fends off the encroaching male mob at Squid Row, a hole-in-the-wall dive with no stage and even less air that was a Seattle mainstay for several years. 1989.*

L7 careened into my living room, *and proceeded to harangue and embarrass me, piss off my roommates and neighbors, and create all-around pandemonium. The craziest, best photo session I've ever made it through. At far bottom left is the cover shot on their legendary Sub Pop single "Shove." Seattle, 1989.*

Kurt Cobain. *Motorsports International Garage, 1990.*

The Fluid (overleaf) from Denver, *put on intensely dynamic shows of the highest energy imaginable. Sub Pop quickly added them to their stable, their first signing outside of Washington State. This Squid Row show was a benefit for them after their van and U-haul were stolen outside my house. That's Mudhoney manager, Bob Whittaker, in midflight on the right. 1989.*

Chris Cornell (Soundgarden) *on stage at Berkeley Square, Berkeley, California, in 1989. Mudhoney opened the show that yielded the photo (left) for Soundgarden's (and the Seattle scene's) major-label debut on A&M, Louder Than Love. The double exposure of the last shot in the series was caused by another photographer's flash going off while my shutter was open. My flash froze his head back, their flash his head forward.*

A motor-drive sequence of Nirvana's finale *at a February 1990 show at Raji's (now defunct) in Los Angeles. This was Kurt's preferred method of ending Nirvana gigs while Chad was their drummer. This sequence yielded two covers: the "Sliver" single (left) and the inner sleeve of the Bleach CD.*

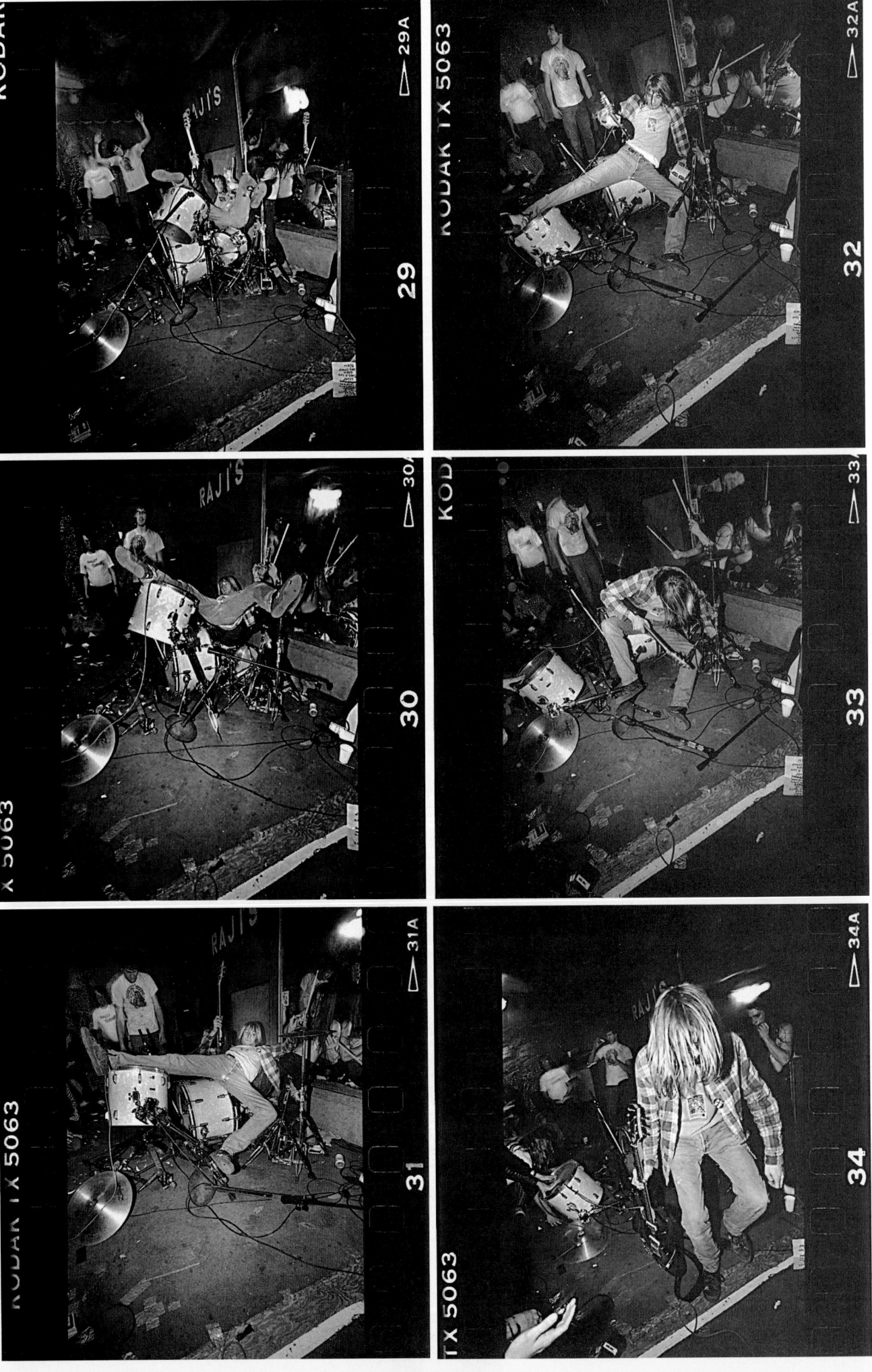

Dale Crover of the Melvins *exiting the stage at RCKNDY. When asked before the show "What is grunge fashion?" by CBS television, Dale dropped his jeans and said, "Well, this is my stage outfit." 1993.*

Buzz Osborne grew up near Aberdeen *along with Crover, Krist, and Kurt from Nirvana, and Matt Lukin from Mudhoney (who played bass in the original Melvins lineup). The Melvins moved to San Francisco in 1988. Grungefest, Cowlitz County Fairgrounds, Washington, May 1993.*

Calvin Johnson of Beat Happening, *an Olympia, Washington, band whose lo-fi D.I.Y. pop ethos greatly influenced Nirvana, Sub Pop, and the entire "international pop underground" community. Beat Happening opened this show for the Melvins at Olympia's Northshore Surf Club in 1992.*

Sonic Youth helped usher the Seattle scene into popularity *with the American underground. They are like respected and endeared older siblings to Mudhoney, Nirvana, and many other groups. Thurston Moore (left) at the Endfest, Kitsap County Fairgrounds, Bremerton, Washington, August 1992. Kim Gordon and Lee Renaldo (above) at the Seattle Center Coliseum, 1991.*

The stage diver at this Mudhoney show *would go on to become famous as "Mr Lifto" from the Jim Rose Circus Side Show. Motorsports International Garage, 1990.*

TAD in the audience. *He would often jump off the stage—always a risky prospect for those up front. The Northshore Surf Club in Olympia, Washington. April 1991.*

Billy Childish playing with his band, Thee Headcoats, *at the Off Ramp in 1991. Childish lives in Kent, England, but was a strong influence on Seattle's garage rock scene; Mudhoney covered his songs and, in 1991, Sub Pop released several of his records, including an anthology that culled one song from each of the fifty albums he had recorded up to that point.*

Kurt Cobain at the Commodore Ballroom in Vancouver, B.C., *opening for the Screaming Trees, April 1991. Note the K sticker on his guitar.*

To celebrate the release of Nevermind, *Nirvana (following pages) played a show at Beehive Records in Seattle's University District. They performed a blistering set to a couple of hundred friends and fans; it's the only time I've seen people clamber on top of one another in a record store. Krist greets the crowd before playing (right). He could almost touch the ceiling. September 1991.*

After playing the in-store appearance, *the band was surrounded by autograph seekers. Kurt seemed terribly overwhelmed by it all, a small portent of the enormous popularity to come. Beehive Records, September 1991.*

Spoofing rumors of his ill health, *Kurt had himself wheeled on stage in a gray wig and hospital gown to an anxious crowd of forty-five thousand at England's premier festival, Reading. Nirvana proceeded to play an absolutely stunning show. Kurt faced a teeming mass of mud-soaked fans (following pages) who sang along to every word. Nirvana's set closed the three-day festival. It would be the last time they played England. August 1992.*

Nirvana's powerhouse drummer, Dave Grohl, *at the Seattle Center Coliseum, September 1992. I rarely get photographs of drummers, preferring to be down in front so as to portray the band from the audience's point of view. Here, however, I was forced to be stageside and turned my camera on Dave. The aftermath (above) of their ruinous finale at Reading.*

Steven Jesse Bernstein *outside his Georgetown apartment in 1990. Jesse was a tattooed Burroughsian poet whose dark prose allied him closely with the Seattle music scene. He opened for many shows, and appeared on the Sub Pop 200 compilation and on a full-length LP for Sub Pop. He took his own life on October 29, 1991.*

Mark Lanegan, *lead singer of the Screaming Trees (far right) and solo singer-songwriter, in the side mirror of my '67 Buick. December 1993.*

The blues-punk supergroup the Monkeywrench. *Left to right: Tom Price (U-Men, Gas Huffer), Mark Arm and Steve Turner (Mudhoney), Tim Kerr (Poison 13, Jack O'Fire), and Martin Bland (Lubricated Goat, Bloodloss). 1992.*

The Fastbacks, a revered and beloved Seattle institution since 1980, *from the session for the "My Letters" sleeve. Note the self-portrait. Left to right: Kurt Bloch, Lulu Gargiulo, Kim Warnick, and Nate Johnson. Mary Ellen's apartment, 1991.*

Kurt Cobain in his Seattle hotel room, New Year's Day, 1993. *After taking some posed photos for the cover of the Advocate, Kurt and I started a conversation. I asked if I could photograph while we talked and he answered in inimitable Kurt style, "Sure. Whatever." He always expressed an intense dislike of having his picture taken, yet he could be very casual and intimate in front of the camera. Kurt seemed exhausted but happy; we talked about his stomach and back pains, about the joy of being a father, and about how he might like to get a house in the Scottish countryside someday.*

Eddie Vedder of Pearl Jam *at Seattle's Magnusson Park, where Pearl Jam staged a free show as a gesture of support to their fans and the community. The city of Seattle tried every means to prevent it, but Pearl Jam (overleaf) prevailed and it turned out to be the largest outdoor concert in Seattle's history.*

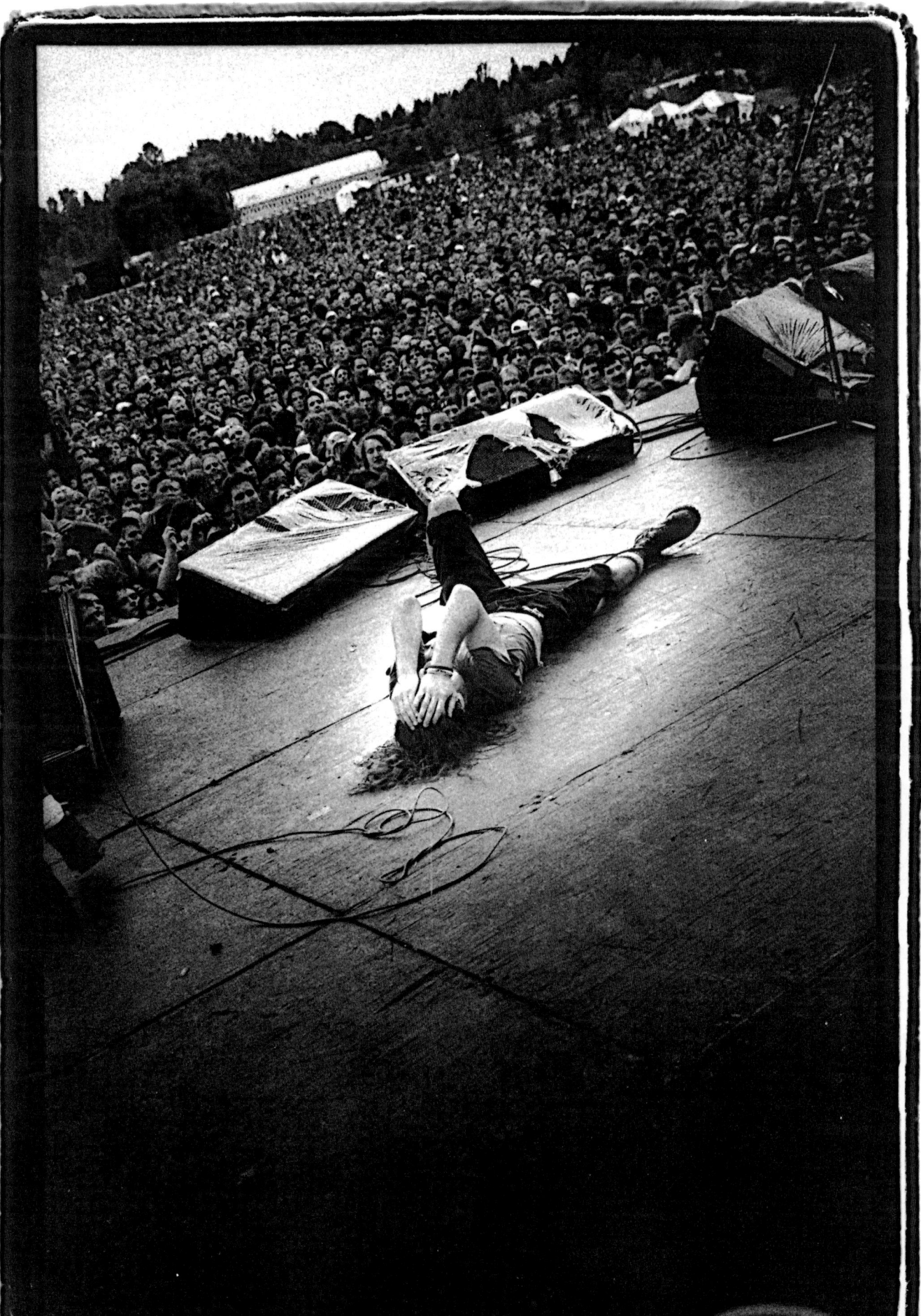

Nirvana opened, unannounced, in October of 1992 for Mudhoney *at Seattle's Crocodile Cafe. Kurt surprised everyone with a stage dive during Mudhoney's set. When he landed back on stage, Krist draped a guitar around his neck and Kurt played punk covers with Mudhoney. That was the last time I photographed Nirvana live.*

Sub Pop graciously took me along for Lamefest Japan *with Supersnazz, Seaweed, the Fastbacks, and the Supersuckers in December of 1993. The reception by the Japanese fans was astounding. It renewed my faith in the vitality of rock and roll. Enthusiasm was the lifeblood of the fans at the Tokyo show (above). Dan Bolton of the Supersuckers in Osaka (right).*

Kurt Bloch (left) is a bona-fide rock star in Japan *along with the rest of his bandmates in the Fastbacks—a sharp contrast to their obscurity in the United States.* **Members of Supersnazz** *(above) amuse Bruce Pavitt's daughter, Iris, on the bullet train to Osaka.*

Seaweed is from Tacoma, Washington. *This photo appeared on their Four album. Grungefest, Cowlitz County Fairgrounds, Washington, May 1993.* **Selene Vigil** *of Seven Year Bitch (right). RCKNDY, January 1993.*

Courtney Love in a surprise set by Hole (left) *that, after a long absence from playing live, left no one with any doubt as to their ferocious power. Crocodile Cafe, 1993. Hole in a candid moment (below). Left to right: Patty Schemel, Kirsten Pfaff, Eric Erlandson, Courtney Love. January 1994.*

Soundgarden during rehearsals *at Avast Studio for their upcoming world tour for Superunknown. December 1993.*

Dave Grohl performing with his post-Nirvana band, the Foo Fighters. *Four hundred people lined the block for this "surprise" show at the Velvet Elvis, which held less than half that. March 1995.* **The teeming mass (overleaf)** *during a set by Mudhoney at the Endfest in August 1992. A far cry from the Central Tavern.*

Acknowledgments

Charles Peterson thanks: Suzannah West. Without her undying love, appreciation, and forthright criticism this book wouldn't have been the same. Michael Azerrad for somehow managing to sum it all up. Jon and Bruce for believing in me. All the bands I have worked with, past and present, for their music and friendship. Special thanks to Nirvana, Pearl Jam, Mudhoney, and Soundgarden for becoming so god-damned famous. Art Chantry for showing me the way. Hank Trotter and Jeff Kleinsmith for knowing what it's all about. Stacy Shelley for making the CD happen. Sarah Lazin for getting this project sold. Joann Moschella and everyone else at Harper Collins for buying it. My family. My friends. My dog, Barkley, for his patience (sort of). Doug Pray for putting me and my photos in his film. Mark Van S. for his consistent generosity (thanks for letting me hog the darkroom). Stefan for his help. Grant and Carl at Vox Populi gallery for giving me my own wall. Peter Bagge for . . . being Peter Bagge. And most importantly, everyone around the world who appreciates my photography. Thank you for your continuing, unselfish support.

Michael Azerrad thanks: Art Chantry, Bruce Pavitt, Jonathan Poneman, and Kim Thayil for their time and wisdom; the Seattle music community for always welcoming this geeky New Yorker; and Charles Peterson for allowing me the honor of contributing to this book.

Photo stuff (for photographers): The 35 mm was done with various Nikon bodies and 16, 20, 24, 35, 50, 85, and 200 mm lenses and various electronic flashes (or not) on Tri-X, T-Max 400, and 3200. The 2 and 1/4 was shot with a Hasselblad and a 40 or 80 mm lens on T-Max 100 and 400. The prints were made by yours truly on Ilford Multigrade fiber base paper. Now go out and do it yourself!

Eddie Vedder *with his trusty Bauer Super-8. Pearl Jam fan club show, the Moore Theatre. February 1995.*